Dear Rwanda

Isabella Mead grew up in Cambridge and holds a Master's in History of Art from the University of York. A former secondary English teacher in East London, she lived and worked for two years from 2010 to 2012 in a rural area of Rwanda with Voluntary Service Overseas, an experience which profoundly informs her writing. She lives in Bristol with her partner and her cat, and is studying for a second BA degree in French, Italian and Spanish. Isabella is Head of Learning and Participation at The Story Museum in Oxford, through which she leads a vibrant team of storytellers and creative writing tutors. She is also a Trustee of Jane Austen House and a Poetry Ambassador at Keats House.

Acknowledgements

With thanks to places in which some of these poems first appeared: 'Rwanda' 'Change' 'Mosquito Net' and 'Kerosene' appear in the *Brotherton Poetry Prize Anthology II, Carcanet, 2022;* 'Angel Trumpets' 'Shakespeare Season' 'Sweetcorn' and 'Tight Rope' appeared in issues of *Poetry News* between 2013 and 2018 and are published on The Poetry Society website; 'Whitewash' was Highly Commended in The Poetry Society's Stanza competition 2019 on the theme of 'Lies', judged by Geraldine Clarkson, and is published on The Poetry Society website; 'Christine' and 'Papyrus' appeared in *Magma 85: Poems for Schools, 2023;* 'Bar Games' was Highly Commended in the Bridport Prize for Poetry 2016, judged by Patience Agbabi, and appears in *The Bridport Prize Anthology, 2016;* 'Genocide Memorial Week' was Highly Commended in the Bridport Prize for Flash Fiction 2019, judged by Kirsty Logan, and appears in *The Bridport Prize Anthology, 2019;* 'African Night' was awarded Runner Up in the Shooter Lit Mag Poetry Competition 2018, and is published on the Shooter Lit Mag website; 'Sunflowers' was awarded First Prize in the Wells Festival of Literature Poetry Competition 2019, judged by Simon Armitage; 'Duracell' was awarded First Prize in the Ver Poetry Competition 2022, judged by John McCullough; 'Rwanda' was awarded First Prize in the Julian Lennon Prize for Poetry 2021, judged by Julian Lennon; 'Rainy Season' was awarded Second Prize in the Segora Poetry Competition 2020, judged by Martyn Crucefix.

With thanks to Chiltern Poets Stanza, Niyonzima Damien, Nigel Ball and Sufi Husain, who helped with drafts of many of these poems.

Contents

Rwanda	4
Change	5
Kerosene	6
Rainy Season	7
Bar Games	8
Genocide Memorial Week	9
Banana Beer	10
Angel Trumpets	11
Sunflowers	12
Sweetcorn	13
Tight Rope	15
African Night	17
My Village Has A New Electricity Pylon	18
Maths Lesson	19
Wedding	20
Goat	21
Whitewash	22
Sugarcane	24
Papyrus	25
Christine	27
Jenga	28
All Our Houses	30
In the Lobby of Hôtel des Mille Collines	31
Shakespeare Season	33
Duracell	34
Slow Stars	35
Mosquito Net	36

Rwanda

Once in a while
a white Toyota
passes briskly through the village,
cuffing potholes.

Children run after
the red rearlights
through rising dust
then settle back

to the sudden gleams
of fireflies
and the smile
of a moon.

Change

Change is precious here, every piece of it.
Time and again it is scooped from a counter,
rubbed free of dust and strands of hair:

francs and cents, festering sediments
exchanged for some sacrifice, along with onions,
phone credit, kerosene, a can of beer.

Children, cupping spiders, pounce on runaways,
the ones that scoot and roll under chairs.
But those who are old enough to remember

turn and turn each coin to the sun,
caress the embossments and serrated edges
with a slow meditation, a tentative reverence.

Meanwhile nuns sweeping the memorial garden
pause to serenade a blue and green beetle:
an impromptu song in unison.

Meanwhile women shelling beans at twilight
never name their silenced virus
but talk of mangoes and rainfall and children.

Meanwhile fatherless men at the bar
practise a dance-step to the latest soundtrack
and praise the cows under the moon at night.

As the praying mantis grips a candle,
transfixed to the flame, so we hold coins:
smatterings of happiness, apertures of light.

Kerosene

Saveri was kerosene, akin to his motorbike,
akin to sunlight over the hills:
pure revs and dust and kerosene,
the jigsaw leaves of banana trees
clattering in the wind. When a tyre gave in
he'd salve the puncture with banana stems
and surge off again in a matter of seconds,
coursing through villages, calling greetings,
kindling the children to clamour attention.
One night of particular rain and wind,
my hut thick with black smoke, he found me,
crying over the mechanics of a kerosene stove.
He threw open the windows and threaded the wicks
in a matter of seconds and set up the burner
in a brisk and passionate affair with vapour.
He doused the viscous grease on my fingers
in kerosene. *It's now your helper, you see?*
Sometimes your enemy is what you need!
In the same breath he told me of his father.
Papa wanjye – khrr - jenoside! - he said,
flicking a finger across his throat
with a guttural choking noise for effect -
I'm sorry, I said – what else - and he laughed,
exclaimed, *No problem!* and touched my arm,
it's OK, he said, *because I forgive them,*
and with that he slipped to the next conversation;
in a matter of seconds was immersed in discussion
on chickens, or beans, or children at sunset
and I remembered the adage, how in Rwanda
peace is more important than justice,
as we dusted the table and shared a beer
through the steadfast lamplight of kerosene
until light overtook the rain and wind.

Rainy Season

The season is defined not by the showers
but the shifts between. After rain
the red earth dries within half an hour
so we venture from the huts again

to the temporary steadiness of the hills.
We gather in a bar for beer and cassava
as a muted hit-single drip-dries from the radio;
Chantal sips Fanta and says *Forgiveness*

is a kind of victory, and in the valley
the children are marshalling the river
to make the most of the swollen flow
breaking in wavelets over the stones,

and Jean de Dieu is playing mancala
with Jean Baptiste whose father years ago
once dragged Jean de Dieu's mother and sister
from the latrine that they were cowering in,

and now they are placing delicate counters
into sunlit bowls, and it doesn't matter
who wins this round as long as the game
ends before the rain starts up again.

Bar Games

5pm. Green Mützig bottles
catch the sun, as District Leaders,
Policemen, Doctors, Government Officials
observe the moves of two opponents.

With easy concentration, twinkling,
Executive cups a handful of marbles
and, working smartly around the board,
plops a marble into each bowl

until he runs out, then claims the heap
he lands upon, and starts again.
Each move is calculated to accumulate 'cows',
vigorous slaps or judicious applause,

clouding the muted discussions in corners
through grey-blue smoke of cigarettes:
the whispered stratagems regarding taxations,
inheritance laws, cooperatives.

The marbles make little chinks against wood:
delicate, sequential, beaded sounds
chiming with the noise of bottles and cash,
the clinks of dreamy acquiescence

echoing the lilt of the stream outside
where children highlight the evening hours
with yellow jerry-cans, then balance back home,
accustomed bare feet on the dusted roads,

towards banana groves and shaded huts
where families, cross-legged, by the goats,
suck banana beer through bamboo
and dip fingers gently into the earth

to form precise bowl-shaped indentations
across the soft ground, and drop in pebbles
to play their version. It's just the same
except that the counters are soundless.

Genocide Memorial Week
Rwanda, April 2011

I stayed in all week. The hut was pervaded with a strange new quietness: a silence stippled with tiny teeth loosening the mud walls by fracturing the whitewash and steadily upturning the earth underneath. A silence infiltrated with insidious clicking and drilling and sucking, like a kind of ruptured tinnitus.

Termites. I couldn't face dealing with them; I didn't want to touch them. Besides, I didn't know where to buy a new pot of whitewash; I'd only been volunteering two months. I didn't know the Kinyarwanda word for 'whitewash.' And it seemed disrespectful to ask my neighbours for advice with such a trivial problem.

So, gently, the termites became entrenched. Their projects bloomed. And I watched.

One night, Baptiste stopped by on his way to a memorial ceremony. 'You will join us?' he asked cordially.

'I – maybe.' I said. He knew I would not. It's not my history, I thought; the West turned its back in 1994; I shouldn't go, out of respect.

So I stayed in. That night, I caught drifts of the ceremony down in the valley: desultory microphones rigged up and holding out even in rain, magnifying the ceaseless reciting of names. And names and names, and now more names.

The next day I ventured out for a walk. I didn't lock the door – no one did. I returned to find my walls newly whitewashed.

'You had an urgent problem,' Baptiste said. 'We came while you were out.'

I did not say thank you, out of respect.

Banana Beer

Alphonsine was queen of banana beer.
Her touch was saved for ceremonies,
graduations, christenings and marriages.
She was queen of the hardened coterie

whose husbands had gone and whose children were silent
yet whose children's children were wildly fine,
scrambled over rivers and ranged through the forests,
learned the Cow-Dance and sang all day.

One evening I tentatively sat down with her.
I was told to just be silent and watch her.
She was unearthing the buried banana skins
coiled under the trees for over a month,

gorgeously absorbing the sweetened soil.
I watched how her eyes started to soften
as if they saw more than banana skins.
I watched her wring droplets into a trough

as twilight fell and the candles shone
and the neighbours gathered, one by one.
Before long they were away with the stars,
murmuring and giggling and singing out names,

until names were all the night became,
a man's name for each woman, and a sip for each name.
I was told not to ask why, but share
the bamboo straw, suck banana beer.

I saw the stars and the moon, no more;
the women sang out names, no more;
while more rested at the roots of the trees,
fermenting with the banana skins.

Angel Trumpets
After Louis MacNeice

There is an abundant flower across Rwanda:
large white chalices that hang from branches
facing downwards, towards the earth.

Maybe a sweet perversity of nature,
perhaps a fear of what the valley might show
or conjecture that bees would not be interested.

Too heavy to stir at footfalls of children
or the steady descent of a bull, they hold themselves
still, like frozen tears or silent bells.

Once, the *umukozi*[1] pulled a few
and stood them in an empty blue Pringles tube:
a centrepiece for guests.

Children stood on tiptoes at the window
for a glimpse of the funny caricature
of the round-faced man with the thick brown beard

from a country where flowers never hide.
The man beamed back across more than just
soundless flowers turned the wrong way up.

---

[1] Housekeeper (Kinyarwanda)

Sunflowers

In dry season Joyeuse leads her classes outside,
teaches Social Studies under sunflowers.
On such days the sun is close,

catches the stipples of grey in her hair
as she leans forward and softens her voice
the way yellow petals spill over seedlings.

The children cluster to answer her questions
between the tendrils and tuberous stalks
and straggled shadows of the framing leaves.

The faces of teachers are threaded with scars.
Joyeuse has only wrinkles. Red dust, though,
can gather in both. The past is close:

there are monuments and textbooks and similar filters.
Yet it sidles guardedly into conversation
only occasionally, and in careful whispers:

*He hid in Congo. Perhaps that is where
he finally rested.* Where? *In the forest.*
Who? *Her husband.* Who? *The Mayor*

- and the words are droplets on lobelia,
rainfall collecting along runnels of creepers,
a crow flapping into a mist. The forest is close:

we can see it from here if we narrow our eyes.
Yet its dense green secrets are far from this dust,
the clicks of teeth, the tickly cough,

the clouded roads, the flaking ligules,
the parched curls of sisal. Between lessons
there are questions, and the answers

seem close. Joyeuse sits in patience
as the hours pass by, playing draughts
against herself, or staring at sunflowers,

their blank faces angled to the sky.

Sweetcorn

They appear at my doorway every morning:
golden parcels, encased in leaves; sometimes
avocadoes, peas. I don't know the reason,
maybe a greeting. I never see him,

but later, perhaps, I'll catch him walking
under banana trees, where the track widens:
the tightened shawl, the careful step, the stick,
as children dip down or run by or high-five:

Papa Fabrice! The traditional custom
of calling a father after his first-born
always stayed with him, though no one knows
a young Fabrice, where he is now.

At the market, I try to catch his eye,
detect a smile - but I'm caught up in greetings,
patriotic songs and praise to the heavens,
pleas for language exchange, conversation -

later, bent over his crop, I see him,
divining the huddled husks in the earth,
twisting the kernels to check for the ripening.
We shake hands, no more. Twenty years ago

he chose to stop speaking. That's the day
no one remembers; eyes will glaze over,
turn to the hills and gaze at the sun.
That night he roasts little pieces of corn

while sounds of the evening crowd the hut:
incessant crickets, the fidgets of wagtails,
the murmurs of cows, the cries of the crows,
mosquitoes crooning the candlelight

and night gives over to swift sequences:
a perfected cartwheel, a rushed row of sums,
lopsided hopscotch, a wash in a stream,
a broken tooth, a falling leaf,

the flash of a satchel or sandals in dust,
the snatch of a laugh. Papa Fabrice
sits on a bench in an empty room,
segments of sweetcorn disassembling the dark.

Tight Rope

The tree trunk that bridged the road and his hut
had weathered to fungus at tissue and heart

yet he never replaced it. He, a master,
could scale the length of it even in rain,

machete in hand, held up like a feather,
jerry-can balanced on a banana leaf crown.

When he'd been at the bar a crowd would gather
to watch him teeter, applaud when he'd land.

At the sound of his singing after dark
children would rush to stand in the water,

arms open, just in case of disaster.
The gleams of fireflies would light his way

intermittently, one then another,
and hearts would falter at the gaps between.

A wavering figure, he'd wobble and giggle,
perform perfected heart-stopping lurches

and always land squarely, both feet together.
His name was Erique, and he could recite

correct rhetoric, and show due disgust
at the doings of his clan, his father.

But beer made him stray off-course sometimes
and on such nights he would start to rail

at unacknowledged acts of violence.
Barmen would dilute his beer with Fanta

and we all tried, all, to watch out for him.
One day someone will hear, we said. He'd grin

and next week we'd be whispering it again;
how, here, our bridges can hold out for years

but can equally soften and give in
at a momentary easing of our fears,

at the slightest coaxing of termites or rain.

African Night

Pylons have yet to stalk the village.
Electricity is a wisp of a word and night
embroiders the wayside undisturbed.

As the sun diminishes, details disappear.
Only the sky reveals its complexities,
its deepening perspectives, signalled by stars.

The hills lose their outlines and close into one.
The roads become even under levelling shadows.
The tea fields tighten. We hold hands home.

Crowded banana trees crosshatch the sky.
The branches fan outwards, balancing shafts
of feathered leaves. Stars filter through.
They are erased by the wind or a fingertip.

Through bunched silhouettes, individual trees
are indistinct, as if to prove
how intimate the world can be
even as the sky expands

My Village Has a New Electricity Pylon

and there was general satisfaction
when it stopped working.

Maths Lesson

Schoolchildren learn to count with bottle caps.
Two Fanta plus three Amstel equals five
and so on, strung across banana-leaf plaits,
stone to stone, an abacus.

Barmen collect them, after closing, for teachers:
bright bits of metal, bouncing and circling
behind rough bar stools. Later, they'll roll
from wooden desks, subtraction in progress,

in a place where time itself is liquid:
meetings start when everyone's arrived
and the bus leaves when it's full; where sunlight
blurs the outlines of crops in haze

and water levels rise and fall
subsumed under seasons' shifting rhythms
and inestimable ageless forces
– no numbers can quantify infinity;

where the amount of stars in the sky depends
upon the shaky geometry of the clouds
and the horizon divides into intersections
which, at times, disappear completely,

as hills flow into one another, and mist
cancels their demarcations again
and children count out bottle caps
in a land of tea and rain.

Wedding

There are always prayers for a cloudy day.
No sunshine, no heat haze, and no blue sky
but absolute whitewash, a sheer hung veil

dispersing all power in the generator,
dwindling down to a crackle of music;
so begins singing, and clapping, and footwork,

the curling procession, the sky so neutral
their colours are kindled: crimson dresses,
golden silks and indigo sashes;

vibrant silhouettes, highlighted figures
bright against the sky, while the clammy air
subdues the dust and softens the path,

smooth for high-heeled step, the gown,
the tread to the chapel. A touch of chill
urges the guests to huddle together

and the vows are crisp against the still, clear air.
The priest blesses the couple with water
and prays that they see green fields forever.

On leaving the churchyard the first droplets start.
Bride and groom open out an umbrella,
tilt it upwards and begin the path.

Goat

Busily, he meticulously inventories the wayside:
grasses, bean-shoots, low-hanging branches,
succinct lines of ants, a postured gecko,
flashes of dust, pellets of dung.

With sudden shakes, plaintive supplications,
he can never have the cow's composure,
the stately amble that owns a pathway,
the level and impassive eyes,

although there may come a moment, when,
lifting his head for a cursory glance
beyond the immediate surroundings, he pauses,
pauses, faces the horizon, acknowledges

a kind of communion with the hills.

Whitewash

Cyprien told me in confidence,
and I promised his secret was safe.
I remember the bar, the tarnished walls,
the termites sucking the whitewash;

their tenacious, implacable persistence
upturning the earth underneath.
We were sucking Fanta through straws.
He was the one neighbour I knew didn't drink.

He leaned forward to utter the words.
I am actually Tutsi. And heartbeats
as the iron roof swelled the sound of the wind,
the men argued louder over the bar,

yet still we worried the termites had heard.
I could almost see them pause,
their drab wings tense as they listened. They didn't.
Perhaps they were in on the secret.

We are all 'Rwandan' now. Not Then.
My grandmother found ID cards of Hutus
after my parents were killed. She carried me
away to this village, where nobody knew us,

and told everyone she was my mother.
One day the people hid in a church
while I led our cows to pasture.
A bit later I heard some screams.

Now the air was still and the men went quiet.
I think they react to the wind.
We looked towards the bar and, reassured,
we talked about termites, terrible things.

I knew the rest: how other survivors
moved ahead with scholarships and stories
and interviews and internships and universities,
while Cyprien still farms for subsistence

then sits in the bar as each evening gathers
collecting the wings that fall from termites,
toying with flakes of whitewash.
He told me this story in confidence

and I promised his secret was safe.
And look at me now, continents away,
sharing this without shame, without even
the courtesy to change his name.

Sugarcane

Chantal ran to sugarcane when she was six,
and hid in the shadows, as she was taught.
She reappeared, unfearingly, and showed them her smile;
she could disarm a soldier, disarm a child.
She could remind them of their little sister.
She could bite them if they tried to approach her.
Scars now crease her cheeks, one on each,
almost exactly in line with her dimples.

She lives. She is sugarcane, if only because
every lunchtime she kneels outside in the dust
slashing fissures in sugarcane with a machete,
sharing out generous slabs with us
so thick we must bite at the waxy surface,
suck hard at the veins and vascular tissue
to draw out the raw juice pooling in sucrose.
It's YOURS now she laughs, as if casting a curse.

Dimples crease Chantal's cheeks, one on each,
almost exactly in line with her scars.
She once slapped a teacher who asked for my number:
He just wants a visa! No one can touch her.
Yet she cannot deny she would like a partner.
I didn't Survive just to live like a Sister!
But I will wait. I am beautiful. I will choose who I marry.
The male teachers smiled. *In Dubai,* she added.

Papyrus

Esperance was saved by papyrus, they say.
I don't know her well, beyond our daily exchange -
Amakuru? Ni meza² – walking together,
amongst sunbirds and warblers. She's an ICT teacher,

conjures computers across wooden benches.
Every morning her students practise the basics,
chalk three miniature squares on each desk
and label each: CTRL, ALT, DELETE.

By rainy season they know the rhythm,
rising through mist, like a benediction:
one finger on CTRL and thumb on ALT,
now, with right index, just dab at DELETE.

A chant: *go CTRL and ALT, go DELETE*
like *Ndasenga Imana,³* like *Rwanda dukunda,⁴*
words she repeated at the age of six
as she stumbled towards the Nyabarongo River.

The river was swamp then, with lumps amongst plants
and the papyrus reeds did not nod in the wind.
The tops were green. She focused upwards
on the star-like clusters, the delicate threads,

ignored the red depths and held her breath.
She held tight to two stalks for ten heartbeats.
Then, swift, caught a chance like the yellow warbler
leaves his perch in an instant, and with a flick,

---

² How are you? I'm fine (Kinyarwanda)
³ I pray to God (Kinyarwanda)
⁴ We love Rwanda (Kinyarwanda)

she ran through the river, barely causing a tremor.
She hasn't told me all this, of course.
It is only ever *Amakuru? Ni meza.*
It was a whispered sentence late at a bar

in the ritual silence that falls between neighbours:
she hid in papyrus in the Nyabarongo River.
Esperance is expecting the laptops soon,
depends on the roads and the rains, and the pylon,

but for now there are desks and pieces of chalk
and soon there'll be Smartphones and WhatsApp and Facetime.
And she will write: *Amakuru? Ni meza.*
And she will say: *Amakuru? Ni meza*

and as for the Nyabarongo River
the yellow warblers still marshal papyrus,
and the reeds are silent and unblemished as ever

Christine
Rwanda, 2019

The war froze her forever at thirteen.
She hadn't yet started her period then,
so every month they hear her screams:
she is ambushed in the dark again.

Otherwise she is lovely mad Christine
sipping milk amongst the chickens,
crocheting legwarmers for cows,
giggling at pretty boys in their teens.

She helps the children with English and Maths,
draws equations in dust with sticks,
asks them why they have no scars,
grips their wrists, strokes their cheeks.

The neighbours smile and say *next year*
when she demands a sip of Primus.
They call her the village's *agakecuru*[5]
which she knows refers to her wisdom.

They are counting the days by the moon
for the arrival, unseen, in the dark.
They place a basin in the schoolyard.
They harden when anyone laughs.

---

[5] Wise, crazy old woman (Kinyarwanda)

Jenga

In cautious candlelight a cluster of families
waited with patience, occasional whispers
and whines of mosquitoes chafing the silence.

It is tradition in Rwanda to visit a newcomer
the very first night, and it is an honour
to receive a neighbour. I did not know,

so, fuzzy from the journey on the pot-holed road,
I waited too, fidgeting, unaware I should offer
the customary beer and Fanta.

And suddenly I remembered the bright suggestion
from the Volunteer Training: the game I had packed
for such a situation, needing no language:

I produced the cheerful yellow Hasbro box
and began the tuition, placing sweet wooden blocks
into neat little levels to a miniature column.

The parents shifted. In time I would learn
of the feared *abarozi*[6] up in the hills,
discover why flowers hung over my door

the night safari-ants spilled from the walls.
But then I knew nothing. On the very first move
the structure shuddered; it all tumbled down

and Mama Seraphine swept up her shawl,
cried *mu rugo!*[7] corralled the children,
furled away with the others following

---

[6] Witches (Kinyarwanda)
[7] Let's go home! (Kinyarwanda)

as a flame from a candle ducked for a second.
Jenga. To build.[8] On the box is written:
Stack it then Crash it! That night I watched films:

the marbled greens of a thousand hills,
the pockmarks of schools and hospitals,
the splintered signage: *Bienvenue!* and *Welcome!*,

as crazed UN trucks charged over potholes
leaving shawls and faces with no words between them;
no houses, just debris where wood beams had fallen.

---

[8] To build (Swahili)

All Our Houses

In 2011, the Rwandan government introduced a scheme to rid Rwanda of all thatched housing. Traditional grass round-huts were destroyed, the Governor of the Southern Province justifying the demolitions by saying 'people were seemingly happy to stay in their thatched houses and showed no commitment to leave them.' Replacement iron-roofed homes were promised, but never organised. Thousands of Batwa families, already the poorest and most marginalised group in Rwandan society, were left homeless.

Music was unspooling from the radio
when the words cut in: *All our houses
will have iron roofs.* And eyes widened through the rain,

figures uncoiled from cross-legged nests
to register the news. That grass-thatched round-huts
were obsolete. *You have one month to move.*

Move from the centre of heartbeat homes,
where whorls of thatch hold a dome of ceiling
over a ring of grass-mats, where an orb of candlelight

licks the ellipses of bottles of Primus,
a bowl of dough-balls, a spiral of marbles,
echoing the cookfire, the plumes of smoke

rising over valleys, while families gather
under a sweeping tree to share news and stories
and cow-dances that mimic curving horns.

Move into a sturdy right-angled unit
where iron sheeting gleams in the sun.
Your new houses are coming. They will arrive soon.

They stood by their homes and when the homes were destroyed
they curled up outside in the slopes of the hills,
the wind-up radio filling the hours.

Yet when the rains set in, they expressed careful hope
new homes would arrive, as if they knew
they'd need corners to shrink into, places to hide.

In the Lobby of Hôtel Des Mille Collines, 31ˢᵗ October 2011

Hôtel des Mille Collines in Kigali was made famous in the film 'Hotel Rwanda'
(2005) as a place of refuge during the Rwanda genocide of 1994. It is now a
thriving haunt of expats bringing Western traditions such as Hallowe'en.

Fresh from their placements, the ghosts file in,
sail through the swing-doors, nod to the porters,
enter 'Private Party', order a whisky.
Their eyes glint with the thought of the prizes,
the ones awarded to all souls, yearly,
for costumes demonstrating sustainability.

Nick from Teach Abroad goes for standard ghost,
doused down in whitewash, clouding the suntan,
face, neck and open chest stunned with powder.
Termites devoured his classroom for weeks,
and only whitewash would smooth them over.

Sandra from Peace Corps burned second-hand books,
rooted for charcoal, splinters of ash,
forked grey gossamer-threads along her biceps,
across her cheeks: a chilling corpse-bride.

> (Meanwhile a bemused waiter in black suit and tie
> passes by, with ripe orange mangoes and knives,
> tea-light candles and boxes of matches).

Lucy from Concern had more imagination,
and incorporated cross-cultural, intergenerational interaction;
she spent a hilarious morning with children
squeezing fat beetles and smearing red juice
in lurid drops down her cheeks as if welling
darkly from her eyes. She makes a good zombie.

Louise from Unicef gathered bottle-caps,
a shimmering range of tinkling metal
in coils of sashes and bangles and bracelets,
the shackles that Marley forged in life
announcing a merrily clinking arrival.

> (Meanwhile a bemused waiter in black suit and tie
> passes by, balancing a blue plastic bowl
> full of avocadoes bobbing in water).

But no one beats Ben from Global Challenge
for facing the paddy-fields in bracing rain at dawn,
hauling up sections of sturdy tarpaulin
for gathering rice. There's enough to stretch
across his whole body, tacked on with Scotch.
He borrowed some pink chalk from a teacher
and drew out the intricate vertebrae,
eye sockets, uneven teeth, a skull's smile.

Shakespeare Season
Rwanda, April 1994

The red dust road opens out to a schoolhouse
where banana trees spread purple flowers
unfurling sunlight, ready to fruit.

In rough-cut classrooms the Hutu children
sing praises to Imana[9] under orders.
The Tutsi children have been sent outside

and stare in silence beyond the yard
through pink angel trumpets and yellow mimosas
at another classroom where Seniors

scratch down verses in exercise books
the same umber glow as the First Folio.
They picture balconies, learn that a rose

by any other name would smell as sweet.
The sunlight sharpens. A gecko settles.
In a few hours the April rains will come,

the flowers will loll, and Romeo bawl,
curl from candlelight into a corner
of a marble portico, sob in the dark

for a message a servant couldn't send;
a stifled UN base in Kigali
will try the New York headquarters again;

there will be no space for new messages
on the answerphone; the schoolhouse will curl
and wilt and blur with the red dust road.

---

[9] God (Kinyarwanda)

Duracell

-the word, spelled out in copper or gold
across two Double-As he holds in his hands:
little cylinders, precise and glossy and smooth

like the cartridge cases or silver bullets
that might have been used in another war
to extinguish a scream in a second, not machetes

making screams endless, endless. A chance
to release the radio's latch in the dark,
slot the batteries into each snug cocoon,

click back the lid, turn on the switch.
Once a day, clockwork, he does just this,
steadies his breathing and listens in

as the soft crackle sharpens to fluid speech,
the latest on roadblocks and military movements
intertwined with music for light relief,

then lists, and every night the names, he
- won't recognise, and tomorrow is saved.
He removes the batteries to a sisal leaf basket, to sleep.

He stretches back amid the intense banana-stench
of fermenting beer, cocooned in the pit
his neighbour dug and hid him in.

She comes to check on him once a day,
drops down a sleeve of plantain, perhaps,
or a sachet of cassava, sunshine gold.

Sometimes, in the darkness, they eyeball each other,
but more often than not he is sleeping.
She drops down to find his heart beating.

Slow Stars

In the Northern Hemisphere, the stars are slow;
it is well known. They take their time:

Venus first, jewel in the sky,
evening star, and then the rest:

calculated scatterings, embellished with names
from epic legends few have read.

Along the equator it isn't like this.
Stars snap on swiftly with the sudden sundown:

late greetings, muted footsteps to mud huts
and mosquitoes start to fuss around the candles

as if even now the night may end.
A plane is shot down at 6pm

and within the hour neighbours are dead
at each other's hands although they prayed together

yesterday, while in the West
we have notice, set the clock;

a mesmerising Venus signals twilight again,
the tail-end of summer evening.

And sometimes when I lean back with the last sips of cocktail,
I can hear the noises, even in England:

the beating of jerry cans, urgent footsteps,
a long, low cry for slow stars.

Mosquito Net

Work is over, and the giving in
echoed in the great unloosening:
reams of netting let down from the ceiling,
tugged taut and tucked in. The world outside
now muted, misty, unimportant,
distances the primitive fear of things:
spiders, scorpions? And worse, perhaps.
Best make the latticework infinitesimal,
allowing just weakened air from the hills,
the sound of cow bells, the fragrance of tea fields.
Dreams, too, may only pass through
once inspected and softened and censored
and blurred into comfort, entering in
with glazed candlelight, with traces of moon.